Eleanor Roosevelt

First Lady *of the* World

By the Editors of TIME For Kids
WITH DINA EL NABLI

HarperCollins*Publishers*

About the Author: Dina El Nabli is the editor of TIME FOR KIDS® online. Eleanor Roosevelt has always been one of her heroes. She hopes the children who read this book, including her nieces and nephews, will be inspired by the incredible spirit with which Eleanor lived.

Library of Congress Cataloging-in-Publication Data is available.
ISBN 0-06-057613-8 (pbk). — ISBN 0-06-057614-6 (trade)

1 2 3 4 5 6 7 8 9 10
First Edition

Copyright © by Time Inc.

TIME FOR KIDS and the Red Border Design are Trademarks of Time Inc. used under license.

Photography and Illustration Credits:
Cover: Yousuf Karsh; cover inset: AP Photo; cover flap: Bettmann—Corbis; title page: Library of Congress; table of contents: Time Life Pictures—Getty Images; p.iv: Franklin D. Roosevelt Presidential Library & Museum; p.1: Time Life Pictures—Getty Images; p.2: The Granger Collection; p.3: Bettmann—Corbis; p.4: Franklin D. Roosevelt Presidential Library & Museum; p.5: Hulton Archive—Getty Images; p.6 (top): Bettmann—Corbis; p.6 (bottom): Bettmann—Corbis; p.7: Bettmann—Corbis; p.8: The National Park Service; p.9: Bettmann—Corbis; p.10: Corbis; p.11 Bettmann—Corbis; p.12: AP Photo; p.13: Lewis Hine—Art Resource; p.14: Oscar White/Corbis; p.15: Franklin D. Roosevelt Presidential Library & Museum; p.16: Franklin D. Roosevelt Presidential Library & Museum; p.17 (top): Bettmann—Corbis; p.17 (bottom): AP Photo; p.18: Bettmann—Corbis; p.19: Corbis; p.20: Corbis; p.21: AP Photo; p.22: Bettmann—Corbis; p.23: Bettmann—Corbis; p.24: Bettmann—Corbis; p.25 Bettmann—Corbis; p.26: AP Photo; p.27: Bettmann—Corbis; p.28: Bettmann—Corbis; p.29: Bettmann—Corbis; p.30: AP Photo; p.31 (top): Corbis; p.31 (bottom): Woman's Bureau—National Archives; p.32: Time Life Pictures—Getty Images; p.33: Franklin D. Roosevelt Presidential Library & Museum; p.34: Time Life Pictures—Getty Images; p.35: Time Life Pictures—Getty Images; p.36: Bettmann—Corbis; p.37: Punchstock; p.38: Bettmann—Corbis; p.39: Bettmann—Corbis; p.40 (top): Bettmann—Corbis; p.40 (bottom): The Granger Collection; p.41: Time Life Pictures—Getty Images; p.42: Patricia Kelly; p.43 (top): Jim Cummins—Corbis; p.43 (bottom): Andrew Wakeford—Getty Images; p.44 (top): Underwood & Underwood/Corbis; p.44 (zipper): Image Bank/Getty Images; p.44 (Snow White): Photofest; p.44 (bottom): Time Life Pictures—Getty Images; back cover: Corbis

Acknowledgments:
For TIME FOR KIDS: Editorial Director: Keith Garton; Editor: Jonathan Rosenbloom; Art Director: Rachel Smith; Designer: Colleen Pidel; Photography Editor: Sandy Perez

 Find out more at www.timeforkids.com/bio/eroosevelt

CONTENTS

"You gain strength, courage, and confidence by every experience in which you really stop to look fear in the face."

—ELEANOR ROOSEVELT

▲ **ELEANOR GOES TO PARIS.** In 1948 Mrs. Roosevelt went to the French capital to talk about the Declaration of Human Rights. Behind her is the Eiffel Tower.

CHAPTER 1

A Voice Heard Around the World

I t was 1948, and Eleanor Roosevelt was in Paris, France. She was about to make a speech for the United Nations, an organization that had been formed only three years before to help settle arguments among different countries. It would be one of the most important speeches of her life.

About 2,500 people packed into a big hall at La Sorbonne, a famous university. World leaders filled the crowd. Newspaper reporters were there to write down her words. Hundreds of others who wanted to hear Eleanor speak couldn't even get in!

▲ ELEANOR appeared on four TIME covers. This one was from 1939.

Eleanor was a confident woman and spoke out for the things she believed in. She was a great listener, too, and wanted to hear from all people—whether they were average citizens or world leaders. But that day the world listened to Eleanor as she made history.

"We stand today at the threshold of a great event both in the life of the United Nations and in the life of mankind," she said. Eleanor had just introduced a new bill of rights that would protect the safety, freedom, and health of people all over the world.

▲ ELEANOR proudly showed off a large copy of her declaration.

UN leaders rose to their feet. The big room filled with applause. Eleanor filled with pride.

Eleanor had come a very long way since her days as a shy girl, when she was afraid of just about everything! As a child, she was scared of the dark, of mice, of basements, of water, of speaking in front of people. She was afraid of not fitting in, not being loved and accepted. Most of all, she was afraid that her family would leave her.

How did Eleanor overcome her fears and become one of the most courageous and important women in American history?

A Shy and Lonely
Childhood

Anna Eleanor Roosevelt was born in New York City on October 11, 1884. She grew up in a big house with nannies, maids, and servants. Everyone called her Eleanor.

Eleanor's father, Elliott, was the younger brother of Theodore Roosevelt, who would serve as President of the United States. Her mother, Anna Hall, was beautiful and popular.

Eleanor had two younger brothers: Elliott (called Ellie) and Gracie Hall (called Hall).

◀ ELEANOR was a shy child.

Even though she came from a rich and important family, Eleanor almost never felt like she fit in. She had buckteeth and didn't smile very much. Her mother

▲ NEW YORK CITY looked like this when Eleanor was a child. The photo was taken in 1889.

thought of Eleanor as an ugly duckling. Sometimes she called her "Granny." Years later Eleanor remembered that she wanted to "sink through the floor in shame." No matter how hard Eleanor tried to please, she still felt her mother didn't love her.

Darling Nell

Eleanor knew she had her father's love. "To him, I was a miracle from heaven," she wrote. Eleanor's fears sometimes disappointed her father, but she tried hard to make him proud. Eleanor loved spending time with him. He called her "darling Nell" after a character in a story by Charles Dickens, a famous author.

Eleanor's father may have been especially proud of her one Thanksgiving when Eleanor was six years old. He took her to help serve Thanksgiving dinner to a group of homeless boys. Eleanor was touched by the

◀ ELLIOTT ROOSEVELT got his kids together for this photo: Eleanor (right), and her two brothers, Ellie (far left) and Hall.

boys' poverty. They taught her an important lesson about helping people in need.

Sadly, Eleanor's father was an alcoholic. His drinking led to many arguments between Eleanor's parents. Elliott Roosevelt spent a lot of time away from home trying to get better. When he was gone, Eleanor was lonely and felt that no one paid attention to her. She couldn't wait to get a letter from her father—or, even better, a visit. He was the most important person in her life.

Tragedy in the Family

When Eleanor was eight, her mother got very sick with a terrible disease called diphtheria. There was no cure for it at the time. Then, on

▶ ANNA HALL ROOSEVELT was a famous beauty.

December 7, 1892, Anna Roosevelt died. Eleanor and her brothers were sent to live with their strict grandmother, Mary Ludlow Hall. Soon afterward, both Ellie and Hall got sick with a disease called scarlet fever. Hall got better, but Ellie didn't. He died in 1893.

Eleanor's father was the only bright spot in her unhappy life. She often dreamed he would come home to take care of her. But on August 14, 1894, Eleanor's father died. That night Eleanor cried herself to sleep.

She refused to believe her father was really gone. Often Eleanor would dream that he was still there beside her. It was the only way for her to deal with the painful loss. But she was soon forced to face the fact that she and Hall had become orphans. Hall was the only close family she had left.

◄ THROUGHOUT her life, Eleanor watched over Hall.

CHAPTER 3

Little Eleanor Grows Up

While living with Grandmother Hall, Eleanor took ballet and piano lessons and spoke French with her maid. She read all kinds of books— from novels and poetry to histories and biographies. She especially loved *Oliver Twist* and other books by Charles Dickens. Eleanor knew a good book could take her to another world.

Summers were spent near Tivoli in upstate New York. Eleanor and Hall stayed with their grandmother in a big house called

▲ OAK HALL, Eleanor's summer home, gave her a sense of belonging.

Oak Hall. On the beautiful grounds, Eleanor played tennis and rode her pony.

Eleanor did not see much of the Roosevelt family. But sometimes she was allowed to visit with her Uncle Theodore, called Teddy, or her two aunts.

Shy Around Boys

When Eleanor was fourteen, she went to a party at her Aunt Corinne's house. Parties like this were painful for her. Because she was taller than most girls her age, Eleanor stood out. Other girls at the party wore long beautiful gowns, but she wore a short out-of-style dress. Her grandmother was still dressing Eleanor like a young girl even though she was becoming a grown-up.

▲ ELEANOR loved horses and horseback riding.

▲ FRANKLIN ROOSEVELT was Eleanor's fifth cousin and childhood friend.

Eleanor wasn't used to dating. So she was very nervous about being at a party with boys. She was happy when a handsome young man named Franklin Delano Roosevelt asked her to dance. Franklin was Eleanor's fifth cousin. After the party, Franklin and Eleanor stayed friends.

When Eleanor was fifteen, Grandmother Hall sent her to Allenswood, an all-girls school in England. Her days were filled with classes, sports, and studying. The students were taught to be good thinkers and problem solvers. Eleanor was learning a lot and making new friends. She even played field hockey! Years later she said the happiest day of her life was when she made the team.

The headmistress at Allenswood, Marie Souvestre, took a special interest in Eleanor. She took her on trips to France and Italy and opened her eyes to a whole new world. Recognizing her student's intelligence and good heart, Marie Souvestre called Eleanor a born leader. For the first time, Eleanor began to feel good about herself.

Coming Home

In 1902 Grandmother Hall ordered Eleanor to come home. Eleanor hated to leave her school. She wished she could stay for a fourth year and begin teaching at Allenswood. The school had done wonders for her. She returned to America a more stylish and confident young woman.

Now that she was eighteen, it was time for her "coming out." That meant Eleanor had to attend a series of parties held for rich girls. The parties were supposed to show members of high society girls who were ready for marriage. Eleanor

▶ WHEN SHE RETURNED to the United States from Allenswood, Eleanor was a confident young woman.

hated these parties and was happy when the social season was finally over. Now she could start doing something far more important to her—volunteering.

Eleanor joined Junior League, a group of wealthy women who did good works. She taught exercise and dance to poor children in New York City. She also joined a group that tried to improve working conditions for women and girls. Many of them toiled long hours in dirty factories with poor lighting and unclean bathrooms.

Wedding Bells

Besides working hard to make life better for others, Eleanor and Franklin Roosevelt were falling in love. When they were apart, they wrote each other letters.

In 1903, twenty-one-year-old Franklin asked Eleanor to marry him. They kept their engagement a secret. Franklin's bossy mother, Sara Delano, said

◄ HERE COMES THE BRIDE!
Eleanor was married in New York City.

they were too young to get married.

Eleanor's favorite uncle, Teddy, was elected President the next year. (Teddy had first become President in 1901, after President William McKinley was killed.) Eleanor and Franklin were thrilled to attend his inauguration. They didn't know that one day there would be another President in the family.

Eleanor and Franklin were married in 1905, on St. Patrick's Day. President Roosevelt gave the bride away, as a father would do. Wedding guests were so eager to see the President that they left Eleanor and Franklin standing all alone at their wedding party!

KIDS at Work

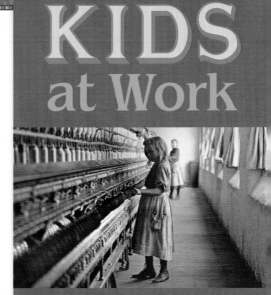

As a young woman, Eleanor Roosevelt tried to make working conditions better for women and children in factories. According to the 1900 census, some two million children under sixteen had jobs in factories, mines, stores, farm fields, and cotton mills. Some kids worked ten hours a day, six days a week for very little money. Many people wanted to outlaw child labor. It was a long struggle to get laws passed to stop kids from working. Finally in 1938, the Fair Labor Standards Act was passed. Child labor was greatly reduced in the U.S.

Eleanor's Exciting New World

After the wedding Eleanor and Franklin settled in New York City. They also spent a lot of time at Franklin's boyhood home in Hyde Park, New York— with Franklin's mother. Sara would often tell Eleanor what to do. In the early years of her marriage, Eleanor made almost no decisions for herself. She tried to please Sara, but Sara was hardly ever happy with Eleanor.

Eleanor and Franklin's family quickly grew. They had three children from 1906 to 1909: Anna, James, and Franklin Jr., who died from the flu soon after he was born. There was nothing

◀ SARA ROOSEVELT and Eleanor never got along. Franklin's mother was tough and demanding.

▲ ELEANOR poses with her children: James, baby Elliot, and Anna.

Eleanor could have done, but she still blamed herself for her son's death. The couple later had three more children: Elliot, Franklin Jr., and John.

The Roosevelts lived in Albany, the state capital, while Franklin served in the New York State senate from 1910 to 1913. When President Woodrow Wilson asked Franklin to be his Assistant Secretary of the Navy, the family moved to Washington, D.C. Eleanor enjoyed life away from Franklin's mother.

She was excited about the opportunities that came with being involved in government. Like other political wives, she gave parties that helped make Franklin better known around town. She also made

▲ ALL ABOARD!
Eleanor and three of Franklin's advisors gave campaign speeches on trains.

friends of her own as she learned more about politics. Eleanor was getting the hang of how things worked in Washington.

In 1920 the Democratic Party chose Franklin to run for vice president with candidate James Cox. Eleanor got a taste of what it was like to campaign for her husband across the country, and she was proud to vote for him. This was the first time women were allowed to vote in an election. However, the Democrats lost.

Eleanor Keeps Franklin Going

The next year tragedy struck. Franklin came down with polio—a disease that left him paralyzed from the waist down. Eleanor took good care of Franklin during

this difficult time. She urged him not to give up. She convinced him to stay in politics.

Franklin was in a wheelchair and could not get around easily. His close advisor, Louis Howe, thought it was important that people did not forget about Franklin while he tried to get better. Howe asked Eleanor to keep

▲ ON THE TRAIL
Eleanor traveled with Franklin as he campaigned across the country.

WOMEN
Win the Vote

In 1920 women won the right to vote when the Nineteenth Amendment to the Constitution passed. Women leaders, including Susan B. Anthony and Elizabeth Cady Stanton, had worked for forty years to win this basic right. They spoke out at meetings, marched in parades, and held demonstrations.

Eleanor was thrilled to be able to vote for the first time. Soon she joined the League of Women Voters, a group that informs people about elections. The league also worked to improve education for women and children. Eleanor quickly became one of its leaders.

Franklin's ideas before the public. He also asked her to be Franklin's eyes and ears across the U.S.

Eleanor wanted to help Franklin, but she shook at the thought of speaking to large groups. Howe coached Eleanor, helping her to be a confident speaker. His advice was very direct: "Be prepared. Know what you want to say. Say it. And sit down. Never appear nervous." When Eleanor learned to relax and control her high-pitched voice, she became an excellent speaker.

Eleanor Everywhere

Traveling around the United States, Eleanor talked to people about Franklin and his goals. She also listened to their problems. As his political helper, Eleanor was becoming more important to Franklin and his career.

However, the busy couple weren't as close as they had been. They began to treat each other as friends rather than as husband and wife. They had a partnership built on respect, admiration, and affection.

Eleanor was also busy with her own work. She remained active in a women's division of the Democratic Party and the Women's Trade Union League, a group that wanted to improve working conditions for females.

With Franklin's help, Eleanor built a cottage called Val-Kill near the family home in Hyde Park. Val-Kill was a place where Eleanor could be alone or could spend time with her close friends. Eleanor and some of her friends started the

◄ ELEANOR enjoyed taking road trips. She was a fast driver at a time when roads were not good.

◄ TODHUNTER STUDENTS loved Eleanor's classes. Eleanor is in the front row, on the right, at the school's graduation.

Val-Kill furniture factory, which created jobs for woodworkers. (Today Val-Kill is a National Historic Site open to visitors.)

Eleanor also helped buy the Todhunter School for girls in New York City, where she taught history, literature, and current events. She always encouraged her students to think for themselves, ask lots of questions, and help others.

Eleanor, the First Lady.

Franklin D. Roosevelt was elected governor of New York in 1928. His health had gotten better, but his legs were still weak. He had to use a wheelchair most of the time. Eleanor kept on working for her husband, traveling to observe the conditions of state hospitals, prisons, and homes for old people. She reported back to her husband on what she had seen.

In 1932 Franklin was back in the national spotlight. Thanks to Eleanor's efforts, voters hadn't forgotten about him. The Democrats nominated Franklin to run for President. He beat Herbert Hoover to become the nation's thirty-second President.

Eleanor was not looking forward to becoming America's First Lady. She didn't want all the attention. But she quickly figured out how to direct it toward the issues she cared about most.

▲ IN THE 1930s, Eleanor helped feed the hungry at a soup kitchen.

A New Kind of
First Lady

J ust two days after Franklin was sworn in as President, Eleanor held her first press conference. She invited only female reporters. This forced some newspapers to hire female journalists for the first time. During her years in the White House, she went on to hold more than three hundred press conferences— a record for a First Lady.

▲ **BY HOLDING** briefings for female reporters, Eleanor hoped to force more papers to hire women.

When Franklin, who was often called FDR during his presidency, took office, the

nation was in the Great Depression. During that time, banks and businesses closed and millions of Americans lost their jobs. People lost their homes because they couldn't pay their mortgages. Many couldn't even afford food. It was a terrible time and, until FDR came to office, most Americans had little hope that life would get better.

During Franklin's first three months in office, he asked Congress to pass a series of laws and programs to lift America out of the depression. The laws and programs together were called the New Deal.

▲ **A COAL MINE** was an ordinary stop for Eleanor as she met with all kinds of people.

Eleanor traveled the country to see the effects of the depression. She was shocked after visiting a mining town in West Virginia. The miners had been without jobs for years. Their families lived in shacks with no toilets. They had little to eat.

Eleanor was determined to help. With government funds, she started a town called Arthurdale for some of the West Virginia miners. Eleanor also gave much of her own money to the community. Soon Arthurdale had new homes and schools. Its residents could get food and health care. Eleanor hoped other towns like it would be built around the country.

With Arthurdale, Eleanor proved to be a strong voice for the poor. Her work earned her admirers across the nation. But not everybody liked her. Some members of Congress said the government was spending too much money on Arthurdale. Others thought Eleanor should mind her own business. This did not stop Eleanor. In fact, it made her more determined to achieve her goal.

Eleanor thought that women could make society better, and so she wrote a book called *It's Up to the Women*. She pushed Franklin to name more women to government jobs. One woman, Frances Perkins, served as Secretary of Labor in FDR's cabinet. (The cabinet is a group of people who run government departments and advise the President.) Perkins was the first female cabinet member.

MYSTERY PERSON

CLUE 1: I was the first woman pilot to fly alone across the Atlantic Ocean in 1932.

CLUE 2: In 1933 I flew over Washington, D.C., with Eleanor Roosevelt. We took turns controlling the plane.

CLUE 3: On July 2, 1937, I was halfway toward my goal of circling the globe when my plane disappeared over the Pacific Ocean.

Who am I?

Eleanor was the first wife of a U.S. President to use her position to accomplish her political goals. During her years at the White House, she was first to:

👉 Advise her husband on political matters and speak out for causes she believed in.

👉 Hold regular press conferences for women reporters.

👉 Give radio addresses and make public speeches.

👉 Write her own newspaper column.

👉 Speak before Congress and the Democratic Presidential Convention.

Reaching Out

Eleanor started writing a newspaper column, called "My Day," in 1935. She wrote about current issues and her life in and out of the White House. Her column appeared in many newspapers across the country, six days a week for nearly thirty years.

As one of FDR's most trusted helpers, Eleanor had a huge influence on the New Deal. She urged her husband to create new government programs, such as the National Youth Administration (NYA). The NYA provided job training for young men and women. By 1936 Americans believed the

New Deal was working. Its important programs helped put millions of people back to work. Americans elected Franklin Delano Roosevelt to another four years as President.

Eleanor's influence continued to grow. She fought against segregation laws, which forced the separation of people by race. In one famous incident, Eleanor quit a group called the Daughters of the American Revolution because it refused to allow black opera singer Marian Anderson to perform in its auditorium. Eleanor arranged for Anderson to give a concert on the steps of the Lincoln Memorial. It was a huge step forward for the civil rights movement.

Through her actions, speeches, and writing, she never stopped fighting for—and giving a voice to—people in need.

▲ THANKS TO ELEANOR, tens of thousands of people heard Marian Anderson sing at the Lincoln Memorial.

The Difficult
War Years

In 1940 FDR became the first president to be elected to a third term. At the time, Adolf Hitler, the Nazi dictator of Germany, was trying to conquer Europe. Much of Europe and Asia was fighting in World War II.

In May 1941, FDR formed the Office of Civilian Defense (OCD). This agency's job was to protect citizens, find volunteers to help the nation, and raise the spirits of the country. Fiorello LaGuardia, the director of the OCD,

◀ELEANOR often spoke on the radio. Thousands of people listened to her.

asked Eleanor to serve as assistant director. At first she turned him down. She worried that her appointment would create trouble for Franklin. Eventually Eleanor changed her mind and took the job. It was the first time a First Lady held an official office in the U.S. government.

America Goes to War

On December 7, 1941, the Japanese attacked the U.S. naval base at Pearl Harbor, Hawaii. The U.S. then declared war on Japan. Eleanor hated war, but as she wrote, "One could no longer do anything but face the fact that this country was in a war."

▲ **THE NEW YORK TIMES** ran this headline after Japan attacked Pearl Harbor.

Eleanor worked hard at the OCD. But Congress did not always agree with the decisions she made. Lawmakers were angry that she hired friends to work for the agency. Eleanor was fed up with all of the people attacking her. So she decided to quit her job in February 1942.

Eleanor wanted to raise the spirits of the country. She began visiting American soldiers both at home and in foreign nations. Her longest trip came in 1943, when she traveled to the South Pacific.

The First Lady spent as much time as she could with the soldiers. She wrote down the names and addresses of the soldiers' families so she could write to them when she returned home. Eleanor knew what it felt like to have a family member fighting in the war. Her four sons were all soldiers.

Eleanor also encouraged women to work outside their homes during the war. She said that factories should have day care centers so women could work without

◄ POSTERS of Rosie the Riveter reminded women to work for victory.

WOMEN

Until World War II began in 1941, the majority of married women stayed at home and raised their families, while their husbands went to work. Most people thought these were the roles that men and women should fill. But Eleanor always believed that women should take part in all areas of work.

During the war, she wrote, "Life in the armed services is hard and uncomfortable, but I think women can stand up under that type of living as well as men."

To help win the war, many women joined the armed forces. They supported the troops as nurses, clerks, and ambulance drivers.

▲ ELEANOR VISITED THOUSANDS of soldiers during the war.

worrying about their kids. She also spoke out about the need for women to be paid the same as men for doing the same job.

IN WARTIME

More than six million women got jobs outside their homes. They built airplanes, worked in steel mills, and drove buses.

After the war, when the men came home, many women went back to being homemakers. But they had proved that they could do jobs that people thought only men could do. However, it would be years before women were a major presence in the workplace.

▲ WOMEN WORKED IN FACTORIES and learned to use big machines.

A Nation's Loss

In 1944 FDR was elected to a record fourth term. By early 1945 World War II was almost over.

However, the war had taken its toll on Franklin, who was exhausted and in poor health. On April 12, 1945, he died at his cottage in Warm Springs, Georgia. Eleanor was in Washington, D.C., when she heard the news. She immediately called Vice President Harry Truman, who would become the new President. Eleanor also sent a message to her soldier sons, who were serving in the war. The telegram said, "Father slept away. He would expect you to finish and carry on your jobs."

The nation was deeply sad over the loss of its President. Eleanor wrote that Franklin was "a symbol of strength and fortitude." After a funeral in Washington, D.C., he was buried in the garden of the family home in Hyde Park.

◀ RESIDENTS OF Warm Springs, Georgia, mourn the death of Franklin Roosevelt.

▲ A SAD ELEANOR attends a memorial service for Franklin Delano Roosevelt.

Eleanor and Franklin had been married for forty years. Now Eleanor was on her own. Speaking to reporters after Franklin's death, she said, "The story is over." She could not have been more wrong.

A Leader for
All People

With Franklin gone, Eleanor was not sure what she would do next. But she knew she wanted to continue making a difference and making the world a better place. In December 1945, a few months after FDR died, President Truman asked Eleanor to serve as an American representative to the newly formed United Nations.

"I believed the United Nations to be the hope for a peaceful world,"

◄ AS THE ONLY FEMALE American representative to the United Nations, Eleanor did not always feel welcome.

▲ ELEANOR traveled to London for the first meeting of the United Nations. The UN later moved its offices to New York City.

Eleanor wrote. She was nervous and excited at the same time. The first meeting of UN representatives was held in January 1946 in London, England.

Eleanor soon discovered she was the only American female representative. "I knew that as the only woman… I was not very welcome," she wrote. But this did not stop her from meeting people and doing her best. There was much reading and planning to be done. She worked eighteen-hour days and devoted all her energy toward improving people's lives and protecting their basic rights.

▲ ELEANOR took part at the opening of the United Nations General Assembly in New York City in 1946. She used headphones to listen to a speech in a foreign language.

Eleanor worked on social, educational, and cultural issues. She also helped refugees—people who were forced to leave their countries during the war.

A Victory for Humanity

In 1947 Eleanor was elected head of the eighteen-nation UN Human Rights Commission. She also was head of a group in charge of writing the Universal Declaration of Human Rights (UDHR).

Eleanor and other UN members worked hard on

the declaration. On December 10, 1948, in Paris, France, she presented it to the UN General Assembly, who would vote on it. The declaration listed the rights of people around the world. These rights included—for the first time in history—the right for all people to be free and equal in all ways under the law. It also stated that everyone has the right to an education.

Getting UN representatives to agree to the declaration was very hard work! When it passed, members of the UN stood up and cheered for Eleanor. Today the UDHR is translated into more than three hundred languages.

The UNITED NATIONS Is Born

In the spring of 1945, World War II had come to an end. Millions of people had lost their lives. Cities in Europe and Asia were destroyed.

Representatives of fifty nations gathered together in San Francisco, California, to work on keeping the peace. On October 24, 1945, they formed a new organization called the United Nations.

The UN aims to settle arguments between nations. It is made up of many departments that try to improve life for the world's people.

Eleanor's Stamp on

History

Eleanor traveled widely in the 1950s to win support for the UN. She also hosted two radio shows and her own TV show, called *Prospects of Mankind*. Eleanor interviewed many important world leaders on the shows, including the civil rights leader Dr. Martin Luther King Jr. and President John F. Kennedy.

Kennedy, a very good friend of Eleanor's, named her head of the President's

▲ LET'S TALK!
Famous people, including John F. Kennedy, appeared on Eleanor's popular TV show.

Commission on the Status of Women in 1961. Now in her seventies, Eleanor continued to speak out for equal rights for women, an important issue that started to get more and more attention.

The Final Years

However, Eleanor's energy was beginning to fade. She was no longer able to keep up her usual busy life. Her doctors discovered she had a serious blood disease.

After spending her seventy-eighth birthday in the hospital, Eleanor wanted to go home. Eleanor's children and friends took good care of her there. She died peacefully in her New York City apartment on November 7, 1962.

▶ ELEANOR posed for this picture shortly before she died.

▲ **FAMILY AND FRIENDS** said good-bye to Eleanor as she was buried beside Franklin. Visitors to Hyde Park can see their graves today.

President John F. Kennedy, former Presidents Harry S. Truman and Dwight D. Eisenhower, and future President Lyndon B. Johnson were among the thousands who went to Eleanor's memorial service in New York City. She was buried in the beautiful gardens surrounding the Roosevelt family home in Hyde Park, beside her husband, Franklin.

▲ **A POSTAGE STAMP** remembering Eleanor was printed after her death.

"I could not at any age be content to take my place in a corner by the fireside and simply look on." —ELEANOR ROOSEVELT

An Incredible Life

Eleanor Roosevelt was a champion for justice who cared deeply about the poor, African Americans, women, and young people. Eleanor wrote more books and newspaper columns, traveled more widely, worked harder for causes, and made more speeches than any other President's wife. No other First Lady in American history has received as many awards and honors as she did. She was a leader who made a difference in people's lives all over the world. Today Eleanor Roosevelt remains one of the world's most admired women. She truly was a First Lady of the World.

Talking About Eleanor

▲ Blanche Wiesen Cook

TIME For Kids editor Dina El Nabli spoke with Blanche Wiesen Cook. She is an expert on Eleanor Roosevelt and has written best-selling books about Eleanor's life.

Q. *Why is Eleanor Roosevelt your favorite subject to write about?*

A. She is an example of what one woman can do. She asked people, "What do you need?" She never tried to tell people what they should think or feel. She was always interested in helping others.

Q. *Why was Eleanor's work so important?*

A. Her goal was to create a better life for all people. Eleanor believed we must know, respect, and trust one another. She believed we must be able to talk with each other.

Q. *How can her life inspire others?*

A. Eleanor was not stopped by tragedy or disagreement. She kept aiming for success.

Q. *If Eleanor were alive today, what do you think she would be fighting for?*

A. She'd be fighting for everything she fought for all her life—peace, justice, health care, and good housing. She'd be fighting for an excellent public education system.

Q. *What advice would she have for kids?*

A. I think she'd say enjoy every moment of your life and find your creative energy—in art, in music, in sports. Talk to each other. And read a lot. Eleanor felt that to read and to know was the key to power.

◄ EXCELLENT HEALTH care for all citizens was one of Eleanor's concerns.

Eleanor Roosevelt's Key Dates

1884	Born on October 11, in New York City
1899	Enrolls at Allenswood School in England
1905	Marries Franklin Roosevelt
1933	Becomes First Lady when FDR is sworn in as President
1935	Begins publishing her "My Day" column
1943	Visits soldiers in the Pacific during WWII
1948	Helps secure passage of the Universal Declaration of Human Rights
1961	Heads the President's Commission on the Status of Women
1962	Dies on November 7, in New York City

1891 The zipper is invented.

1937 Disney's first full-length animated feature, *Snow White and the Seven Dwarfs*, opens.

1959 Hawaii and Alaska become states.

STATEHOOD!